Weird, Weird World

Weird, Weird World

by Mary Packard

and the Editors of Ripley Entertainment Inc.

illustrations by Leanne Franson

SCHOLASTIC INC.

New York   Toronto   London   Auckland   Sydney
Mexico City   New Delhi   Hong Kong   Buenos Aires

Developed by Nancy Hall, Inc.
Designed by R studio T
Cover design by Atif Toor
Photo research by Laura Miller

ISBN 0-439-63368-0

Printed in the U.S.A.
First printing, January 2004

Contents

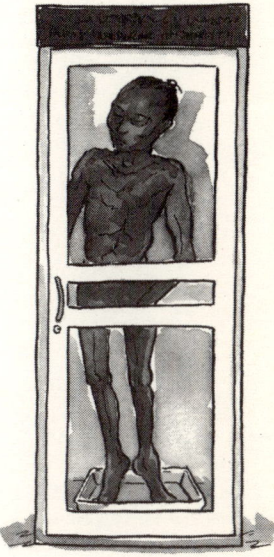

Weird, Weird World

Introduction

Everywhere and All the Time

Robert Ripley became an overnight success with the publication of his first Believe It or Not! cartoon in the *New York Globe* on December 18, 1918. By 1929, Ripley was one of the top cartoonists in the country, with his work appearing in more than 200 newspapers in the United States and Canada alone. It was not just the drawings that attracted his readers but the stories behind them as well.

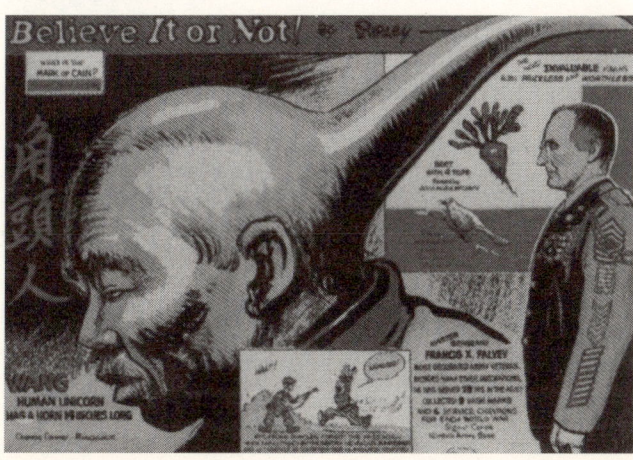

Anything weird, creepy, or bizarre enough to get Ripley's attention found a place in the files of Believe It or Not! And the amazing truth is that Ripley never ran out of material. He was able to supply at least three outrageous stories every day for 30 years—each one more unbelievable than the last. When asked, "Where do you get all your facts?" Ripley had a quick reply: "Everywhere and all the time."

For weirdness, it would be hard to top the Kapsiki tribe, whose blacksmiths carried the corpses of wealthy people on their shoulders and gave them dancing lessons in preparation for the good life in the next world. Then there are strange news stories—like the one about the thief who got stuck in the chimney of the restaurant he was robbing and another about the zoo owners whose maid of honor and best man were tigers.

In *Weird, Weird, World,* you'll find out about the Slovakian custom of shaping beehives to resemble the beekeeper and his wife, the French shepherds who patrol their land on stilts, and the American cowboys who use

helicopters to herd their
cattle. You'll see a huge
mosque made out of
mud and a former hotel
shaped like an elephant.
Equally strange are
natural structures, like
the rock formation that
looks like a hamburger.

Though the stories in *Weird, Weird World* may vary
greatly in subject matter, they all have two things in
common: They are really weird and they are really true.
See just how much weirdness you can believe by taking
the How Weird! and Brain Buster quizzes in each
chapter. Then try the special Pop Quiz at the end of
the book and figure out your Ripley's rank with the
handy scorecard.

When you are through, you just might end up
agreeing with Robert Ripley, who said, "I don't blame
anyone for thinking me a liar because there's nothing
stranger than the truth."

Believe It!®

Rituals and customs vary from culture to culture and from one century to the next— which just goes to show that there is always more than one way of doing things.

Splat! It was once the custom of people living in the Ozark Mountains to squash the first louse they found on a child's head with a tin cup if they wanted that child to be a dancer.

How Weird!

Each year in Caryville, Florida, there is a contest to see which fiddler can . . .

a. play the longest.
b. make the most dogs howl.
c. draw the most worms out of the ground.
d. put the most people to sleep.

Monkey Business:

An ancient Egyptian painting indicates that 4,000 years ago, baboons were taught to harvest figs. Today, in Southeast Asia, pigtailed macaque monkeys are trained to scurry up trees to harvest coconuts.

Working Under Cover: While harvesting rice, women of Honshu, Japan, still wear the same style masks they first wore centuries ago to make them unattractive to male supervisors. Now, however, the masks are used to protect them from insects and sunburn.

Web Sight-ings:

Women in Madagascar can be seen gathering the webs of nephila orb weaver spiders and spinning the threads into textiles.

Planes on the Range: The 1,300-square-mile King Ranch in Texas has 2,730 oil wells and 60,000 head of cattle that are herded by cowboys in helicopters.

How Weird!

To protect their crops from ants and animals, farmers in the Orinoco forests of South America . . .

a. plant their crops indoors.
b. place booby traps in their fields.
c. line their fields with sticky flypaper.
d. plant their crops in boats set high above the ground.

Bewitched: In order to increase milk production in their cows, Polish peasants ritually pour milk through the hole of a wooden charm called a cow bewitcher.

You Look Familiar: Slovakian beehives are carved to resemble the beekeeper and his wife. Why? So that the bees will recognize their owners.

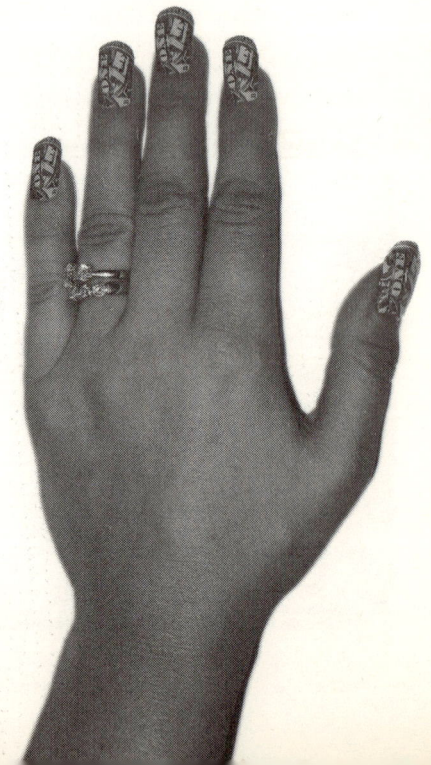

Cash Tip: A certain nail fashion involves a manicure in which pieces of money are cut up and applied directly to fingernails (*right*).

Golden Tip-off: Ancient Chinese nobles grew their fingernails to great lengths to show their rank. To keep the nails from breaking, they protected them with carved gold nail guards.

High Stepping:

In order to keep a sharp eye on their flocks of sheep, shepherds in Mont-de-Marsan, France, patrol their land on stilts equipped with antifog lights.

Bracing Custom:

In Scotland, farmers frequently put braces on the teeth of sheep!

How Weird!

Because they believed that eating this food would prevent people from getting drunk, the ancient Egyptians actually built monuments to . . .

a. cabbage.
b. wheat.
c. fish.
d. tomatoes.

Feeling Sheepish:

In the town of Culembourg, The Netherlands, six sheep are let loose in the streets to control the speed of rush-hour traffic.

Good Seeds:

Natives of the West Indies carry seeds of the yellow oleander, also called the "lucky nut" plant, for good luck. They even place the seeds in the hands of newborn babies to bring them good fortune. However, they don't eat the seeds—or any part of the plant—because they are poisonous.

Charmed: Good-luck charms were once written by Taoist priests in China as a means of curing disease. The patient burned the formula and swallowed the ashes.

Hot Feet:

In India, more than 5,000 people a year walk through flames in the belief that it will assure the speedy recovery of sick relatives—yet not one person has ever suffered burns.

Hard to Grasp! Among the Thais of Vietnam, a baby boy must decide what career he will pursue by his first birthday. Symbols of various occupations are placed in front of him, and the first object he grasps will determine his life's work.

For Crying Out Loud: A baby that is born to the Akha people of Thailand cannot be touched until it has cried three times.

Bone-ified Baby Gifts: It was once customary for the godmother of a baby born to the Yahgan people of Tierra del Fuego, South America, to give her godchild two hollow bird bones: one to use as a straw to drink from and the other to use as a back scratcher.

Illegal Lashes:

In Morrisville, Pennsylvania, it was once against the law for women to wear mascara or any other kind of makeup—including rouge, lipstick, and eye shadow— without a permit.

Walking Tall:

Teenagers in the Sudan wear a headdress with three shells dangling in front of their face. To keep the shells from bouncing against their noses, they have acquired beautiful posture and glide gracefully wherever they go.

A Furry Fiancé:

According to the beliefs of the Santhal people of Bengal, India, a child must be married quickly to break what they consider to be an evil spell. This is exactly what happened when the parents of nine-year-old Karnamoni Handsa discovered that one of the girl's teeth had grown in on her upper gum. The parents considered this a bad omen, but since they did not have enough money for a proper wedding, they conducted a mock ceremony in which their daughter was married to a dog. Luckily for her, Karnamoni is still free to marry when she grows up and does not have to divorce the pup!

How Weird!

In the 1750s, breeches were worn so tight in Alexandria, Virginia, that the men . . .

a. had to climb on a raised platform to get into them.
b. hired children to follow them and tell them if their seams were about to split.
c. often passed out from the tight girdles they wore underneath.
d. were prone to excessive dieting.

Free-for-all: People on the Island of Nauru in the Pacific Ocean practice a custom called *bubutsi* in which anyone who admires anything automatically receives it as a gift.

No Pain, No Gain: This man is wearing the traditional tattoos and dress of a Maori tribal leader of New Zealand. At one time, Maori tribal leaders were elaborately tattooed by breaking the skin with a chisel made of albatross bone. A dye was then injected into the wound. The reward for the pain was great respect. After the tribal leaders died, their tattooed heads were removed and preserved as a tribute to their bravery.

Bad Hair Days: Many ancient marriage rituals were all about hair. At Russian weddings, the bride's hair was sprinkled with a mixture of oats, barley, and linseed oil. In Abyssinia, locks of the bride's and groom's hair were dipped in honey and water and glued to each other's head. In ancient Rome, the groom combed the bride's hair with his spear to frighten away evil spirits.

How Weird!

In 19th-century Borneo, when a person died, the body was . . .

a. squeezed into a jar and kept there for a year.
b. cremated.
c. buried at sea.
d. buried beneath the home of his or her closest relative.

Pulling Strings: The people of Easter Island tell stories using string figures called kai-kai. They shape the string with their fingers, like the western children's game of cat's cradle.

Their Name Is Mud: The mud men of the Asaro Valley in Papua New Guinea cake their bodies with mud and wear grotesque masks fashioned from mud. They once did this to frighten their enemies, but now they do it to entertain the tourists.

Flea Collar Chic: In the 16th century, upper-class women often wore "flea furs" around their shoulders to attract and trap fleas so that the critters wouldn't bite them!

No Shelf Life: Lady Gough, a distinguished upper-class woman who lived in England during the Victorian era, wrote a book of etiquette in 1863. This example of her advice appears on page 105: "The perfect hostess will see to it that the works of male and female authors are properly separated on her bookshelves. Their proximity, unless they happen to be married, should not be tolerated."

How Weird!

In 1933, the chief of the Parisian police asked actress Marlene Dietrich to leave Paris for going against the custom of the day. Her crime was . . .

a. walking a German shepherd in a French city.
b. wearing pants in public.
c. not wearing a hat on Bastille Day.
d. driving on the wrong side of the road.

Chipping Away: Aborigine men of the Gibson Desert in Australia are the only people on Earth who create stone tools and weapons by shaping rocks with their teeth.

Gold Toast: For more than 350 years, the mayor of Grammont, Belgium, and every member of his town council were required once a year to drink a cup of wine containing a live goldfish!

Stuffy Custom: In Africa, a widow of the Tikar people must wear two buttons from her deceased husband's clothing in her nostrils as a gesture of mourning.

Silent Partner:

In the Kapsiki tribe of Africa, a wealthy person who dies is given a head start on the good life that Kapsikis believe a person of standing should live in the next world. The village blacksmith hoists the corpse onto his shoulders and gives it dancing lessons that last for hours!

Soul-full:
In the north of Scotland, some people consider it sinful to kill a butterfly because they believe that these insects carry the souls of lonely people who have died.

Stiff Rules:

When a family member dies, the Igorots of the Philippines stage a month-long banquet with the corpse propped in a chair as the guest of honor.

How Weird!

Until the 1800s, the Tlingit people of Alaska cremated all their dead except shamans because they believed . . .

a. cremated shamans would come back to haunt them.
b. shamans would not burn.
c. the burial site of a shaman would always be fertile.
d. a shaman's ashes would poison the ground.

Good Spirits:

The Uape Indians of the Upper Amazon in South America drink the ashes of their dead mixed with casiri, a local beverage, in the belief that they will absorb all the good qualities of the deceased.

Roach Catchers:

People in Thailand kept cockroaches as pets—until the health department began cracking down on the practice. Calling the cockroaches pests, officials confiscated and destroyed about 1,000 roaches. To make up for the loss, they held a public funeral for them!

Handy Bugs:

Some animal lovers in Australia also keep pet cockroaches. But they're not just ordinary cockroaches. They're wingless Australian burrowing cockroaches—and they're as big as the palm of your hand! (*See color insert.*)

What are the advantages of having one of these monsters for a pet? They don't fetch or roll over, but on the other hand, they don't bite, they're not fussy eaters, and they don't need to be taken for a walk in the rain at 5:00 in the morning.

How Weird!

In China, people rent dogs at a rate of 23 cents for 10 minutes because . . .

a. it's illegal to own a dog in China.

b. Asian breeds are extremely expensive to buy.

c. there are not enough dogs to go around.

d. dogs are worshiped in China.

Sure, it's a weird world out there! But can you tell the difference between what's *really* weird and what's not only weird but *unreal?*

Robert Ripley dedicated his life to seeking out the bizarre and unusual. But every unbelievable thing he recorded was known to be true. In the Brain Buster at the end of every chapter, you'll play Ripley's role—trying to verify the fantastic facts presented. Each Ripley's Brain Buster contains a group of four shocking statements. But of these so-called "facts," **one** is **fiction**. Will you **Believe It!** or **Not!**?

Wait—there's more! Following the Brain Busters are special bonus questions where you can earn extra points! Keep score by flipping to the end of the book for the answer key and a scorecard.

Every culture has its own way of remembering the dead. Can you tell the difference between the rituals that are really practiced in different countries and the one that is dead wrong?

a. On the holiday of Famadihana in Madagascar, loved ones are removed from their tombs, filled in on family gossip, and danced with before they are returned to their graves.

Believe It!   **Not!**

b. In ancient Greece, it was taboo to mention an animal at a funeral for fear that the deceased would return to Earth in that animal's form.

Believe It!   **Not!**

c. The Batak warriors of Sumatra carried life-sized wooden puppets, carved in the likeness of the deceased and fitted with sponges in the eyes, to ward off evil spirits at funerals.

Believe It!   **Not!**

d. In ancient Egypt, cats were mummified and buried with their owners.

Believe It!   **Not!**

• •

BONUS QUESTION

Spines of the sea urchin are used on the Pacific Island of Rarotonga as . . .

a. flutes.

b. wind chimes.

c. pencils.

d. hair ornaments.

From the fantastic to the fantastical, the structures in the following pages are guaranteed to amaze and delight.

Earth, Sweat, and Years: The Great Wall of China is about 25 feet tall and wide enough for ten people to walk side by side. Spanning 4,000 miles of mountainous terrain in northern China, it is large enough to make an 8-foot-long, 3-foot-thick belt to wrap around Earth's middle. Constructed entirely by hand out of earth, stone, and bricks, it took workers hundreds of years to build! Many of the laborers died during its construction, and some are buried in the wall.

How Weird!

The palace of the Marsh Arabs in Saudi Arabia has huge archways made out of . . .

a. camel bones.
b. clam shells.
c. bundles of rushes.
d. clay.

Bridge to the Future: In 1502, Leonardo da Vinci drew up plans for a bridge to connect the European and Asian sides of Istanbul, Turkey. But the bridge was never built because the Turkish ruler thought the design would never work. Five hundred years later, in 2001, the plans were rediscovered by artist Vebjørn Sand, who was able to get the bridge built in As, Norway. Sand hopes to build a Leonardo-style bridge on every continent as a symbol that "you can make anything you dream a reality."

Squeaking By: The Somerset Bridge in Bermuda is the world's narrowest drawbridge. It has an 18-inch-wide flap that raises to allow the masts of sailboats to pass through.

Perfect Pitch: Designed 2,000 years ago by Greek architects, a theater in Aspendos, Turkey, is so acoustically perfect that every word spoken on its stage can be heard clearly in any of its 13,000 seats.

Jet-Sitters: Marcus Sitticus, the 17th-century prince-archbishop of Salzburg, Austria, had water jets installed on the stools around his palace courtyard as a practical joke to surprise his unsuspecting guests. Four hundred years later, they still work.

Sole-full: In 1948, shoe executive Mahlon Haines of Hellam, Pennsylvania, built a three-bedroom house with two bathrooms that just happened to be in the shape of a shoe.

Pachyderm Pavilion: In 1882, James T. Lafferty built a hotel in the shape of an elephant. Nicknamed Lucy, this historical landmark is now located in Margate, New Jersey. Lucy is 65 feet tall and weighs 90 tons. For $4 you can wander through its pink rooms and get an elephant's-eye view of the city.

Air-Tight Blessings: For those who would like a church wedding but would also like to get married at an out-of-the-way place such as a beach or on top of a mountain, the inflatable church is just the thing. Blow it up, and a church suddenly appears, complete with steeple, stained-glass windows, pews, and even inflatable candles. You can buy your own inflatable church for $48,000 or rent it for $4,400 a day. Clergy is extra.

Magnificent Mud: The largest mud-brick building in the world can be found in Mali. The Grand Mosque of Djenné was built in 1906, modeled on the design of an earlier mosque built in the 1200s. The wood spikes almost make it look like a fort instead of a mosque, but they're only there to support the mud. The townspeople spend about one month a year after the rainy season fixing the smooth outer layer of mud and making any other repairs that are needed.

How Weird!

The lower two floors of a three-story house on Herkimer Street in Albany, New York, were . . .

a. stolen.
b. covered with bottle tops.
c. plastered with seashells.
d. built around a playground.

Holy Recycling: The 242-foot-high Wat Arun temple in Bangkok, Thailand, was built out of broken dishes salvaged from a shipwreck.

The Fragrant Minaret:

The Koutoubia, an 800-year-old tower in Marrakesh, Morocco, was built with mortar mixed with 900 bags of musk so that the holy building would always smell like perfume.

Rock of Ages: Pilgrims have to climb rickety ladders and scaffolding to reach the Maijishan Grottoes, 194 temples carved out of the solid rock of a steep 466-foot-high hill in China. In the grottoes are more than 7,000 clay sculptures and more than 10,000 square feet of murals. Work began on the grottoes in the late fourth century and continued until the 1800s.

Gift from the Sea: A tiny chapel (*right*) on the Isle of Guernsey in Great Britain was made entirely out of seashells and broken pottery.

Instant Laugh Track: Stand-up comics might enjoy performing in the Whispering Gallery located in the dome of Gol-Gumbaz in Bijapur, India. Why? Because within those walls, laughter produces more than twice the number of echoes than those that are produced by other sounds!

How Weird!

One part of the Statue of Liberty that weighs 100 pounds is . . .

a. the torch.
b. the crown.
c. one big toe.
d. one fingernail.

Shell Shock-Proof: The Castillo de San Marcos in St. Augustine, Florida, a star-shaped fort built in the late 1600s, is constructed partially of seashells. Despite numerous attacks on the fort, it has never been taken by military force.

Stairway to Heaven: When work on the Loretto Chapel in Santa Fe, New Mexico, was finished in the early 1870s, there was one thing missing: a staircase to the 22-foot-high choir loft. Given the small size of the chapel, a regular staircase would have taken up much of one side. It seemed the only other choice was a ladder. Then an old gray-haired man with a toolbox appeared at the chapel and offered to build a staircase, but only if his name was never revealed. Once the beautiful circular staircase was finished, he simply disappeared. Some say he was really Saint Joseph, but even if he wasn't, his "Miraculous Staircase" is still a wonder. Held together with only wooden pegs, the staircase makes two 360-degree turns—without any center support at all.

How Weird!

Mezhirich, a town in the Ukraine, was built 15,000 years ago with houses made entirely of . . .

a. vodka bottles.
b. lava.
c. mammoth bones.
d. pebbles.

Head-Quarters: The inside of the octagonal Armour-Stiner house in Irvington, New York, represents a human brain. Its rooms were laid out according to the principles of phrenology, the pseudoscience that maintains that bumps on the head have an effect on personality.

Fish Out of Water: Part of the National Fresh Water Fishing Hall of Fame in Hayward, Wisconsin, is built in the shape of a leaping fish. The "fish" is half a city block long and four-and-a-half stories high. Its open mouth serves as an observation platform!

Most Breakable: Tressa "Grandma" Prisbrey visited the dump every day from 1951 to 1981, picking up discarded bottles. What did she do with them? She built Bottle Village, a fantasy of shrines, wishing wells, child-sized buildings—and even a Leaning Tower of Bottle Village. How did it start? She wanted a place to store her collection of 17,000 pencils!

Pig Heaven: In 1891, the Squire of Flying Hall, North Yorkshire, England, built a giant pigsty in the shape of a Greek temple complete with carved Ionic columns.

Crooked Corner: Herman de Wall's home in Utrecht, Holland, has no straight walls.

How Weird!

A house near Sweetgrass, Montana, has a bedroom . . .

a. in the United States and the kitchen in Canada.
b. that is divided by a huge tree.
c. that's built around a skating rink.
d. for the owner's favorite pet prairie dog.

Be-Doodled:

One side of an apartment house owned by Mark Van Noppen and Tyler Roberts in Providence, Rhode Island, was given an elaborate color-by-number look that included crayon scrawls and three 17-foot crayons.

Can You Dig It?

Had Baldasare Forestiere seen his land in Fresno, California, before he bought it in 1905, he might have changed his mind. Nothing would grow in its hard, sunbaked dirt. But Forestiere hadn't worked digging subways in the East for nothing. He dug right in and didn't stop until he died in 1946. By then, he'd dug a 90-room underground house, complete with skylights, fruit trees, gardens—and even an overhead aquarium.

It's Melting!

A building in Odeillo, France, which was designed to tap solar energy for heat and light, looks as if it's actually dissolving.

Monsters in the Woods:

In the 16th century, Vicino Orcini made plans for a garden in Bomarzo, a small town in the province of Viterbo, Italy. He called it *Bosco Sacro,* or sacred grove, and had it filled with sculptures of monsters and fantastical animals carved out of boulders. One monster is so large, a person can walk into its mouth.

But Can It Cook?

A computerized house in Ahwatukee, Arizona, can turn on its own lights, talk to its owners, and help prepare a grocery list.

How Weird!

A home at Lexington Avenue and 82nd Street in New York City was four stories tall but only 5 feet wide at each end. It was built by Joseph Richardson to . . .

a. provide shelter for homeless little people.
b. spy on his neighbors.
c. block his next-door neighbor's view.
d. serve as a movie set.

Ripley's Believe It or Not! Brain Buster

These wacky inns are really far out. Three of them actually exist. Can you spot the inn that is so far out it's unreal?

a. Jules' Undersea Lodge in Florida is a hotel built below the ocean's surface. Guests can view marine life and scuba divers while they relax in bed.

Believe It!   Not!

b. The Sleepytime Inn is a 20-room hotel in Pasadena, California, where sweet dreams are guaranteed. The beds are shaped like clouds.

Believe It!   Not!

c. Treetops is a resort in Kenya, Africa. Its first visitors in 1932 had to climb a wild fig tree to reach their room. One famous visitor climbed the tree one night in 1952 and descended the next morning as Queen Elizabeth II of England. During the night, the king, her father, had died.

Believe It!   Not!

d. At the Ice Hotel in Sweden, the temperature in the master suites is five degrees above zero.

Believe It!   Not!

BONUS QUESTION

A pyramid-shaped structure owned by a Waukegan, Illinois, developer . . .

a. swivels on its axis so that it always faces the sun.

b. is entirely covered with 24-carat gold.

c. is even larger than Egypt's Great Pyramid.

d. has a stable for 25 camels.

3 Totally Out There

There is no end to the weird people, places, and things in this world. To find them, all you have to do is read the news.

Cowboy Underpants:

In New York City, it is not unusual to see people who are a little offbeat. What *is* unusual is for passersby to notice them. But when Robert John Burck, who calls himself The Naked Cowboy, takes to the streets, people actually stop and stare. That's because this street performer does his act wearing nothing but a cowboy hat, a pair of cowboy boots—and white underpants!

How Weird!

In Caroga Lake, New York, there is an annual . . .

a. smelly sneaker contest.
b. race in which competitors pull wooden outhouses through the snow.
c. race in which contestants push their partners seated on sofas down the street.
d. contest to see who can hug the most trees.

Puppy Love: Little Tatiana Anjelica and Tyson Beckford Spak were married on June 2, 2003, in Derby, Connecticut. With tails wagging and dressed to the teeth, the dogs could barely contain their excitement as they shared a wedding cake made out of dog food and cheese snacks. The groom wore a top hat and a tuxedo, while the bride wore a veil and a tiny garter on her paw. Ten of their best canine pals shared in the festivities.

Vowing Deeply: In June 2003, Chandan Thakoor and Dipti Pradhan of India got married in a most unusual way. Over their traditional wedding clothes, the couple, the wedding party, and the priest strapped on oxygen tanks so they could last the 38 minutes it took to perform the ceremony underwater!

Purr-fect Wedding: Eileen Oren is the owner of ME's Zoo, 50 miles northeast of Indianapolis. So when she and her fiancé, Bob Taylor, got engaged, they decided to hold the wedding at the only place that would allow their best friends to serve as attendants—the zoo! The best man was Bobbi, a male tiger, and the maid of honor was Massai, a female tiger. Omar, the camel, served as the ring bearer. A wild time was had by all.

How Weird!

As protection against witches and demons, brides once . . .

a. carried bouquets of garlic, chives, and rosemary.
b. wore headdresses fashioned from wild onions.
c. wore bracelets made of eggshells.
d. wore pouches of mouse ashes around their waists.

Cat-chy Idea: If your feline companion is taking too many catnaps, and her only reaction to her cat toys is a big, fat yawn, *Meow TV* may be just what the doctor ordered. Sponsored by Meow Mix, *Meow TV* bills itself as a "show for cats and the people they tolerate." With videos of squirrels and fish and segments such as "Kitty Yoga" and "Cat Haiku," *Meow TV* is guaranteed to put an end to kitty boredom for good.

Eeeeek! Every year, Nebraska Wesleyan University hosts The Event Formerly Known as the Rat Olympics. Rats compete in such events as the long jump, weight lifting, and the 5-foot rope climb!

Rodent Rituals:

Each year, thousands of faithful Hindus from around the world journey to the province of Rajasthan, India, to visit the Karni Mata Temple and pay tribute to its sacred rats. The ornate temple is crawling with the rodents, which flock to the large bowls of milk and food scattered throughout the temple. Many people offer the

beady-eyed ones food from their hands. If a rat accepts the food, good luck will follow. The best luck, however, comes if someone spots one of the few white rats on the premises. Why are the rats sacred? It's said that they are inhabited by the souls of storytellers, who in their next lives will be human once more.

How Weird!

Romania's prime minister has announced plans to build a . . .

a. Dracula theme park.
b. vampire museum.
c. werewolf safari park.
d. vampire-proof graveyard.

Ho, Ho, Ho! In June 2003, a would-be burglar got stuck in the chimney of Luigi's Italian Cuisine in Jackson Heights, New York. He used a garden hose to rappel down the chimney but got stuck when the hose broke. It took police two hours to smash through the bricks to get the suspect out of the tight spot he was in. Then they arrested him.

Unsightly! In May 2003, 30-year Remi Tsolakis was arrested at Athens International Airport in Greece when authorities learned he was wanted in Rhodes for a minor offense. To protest his arrest, the man forced his eyes so far out of their sockets that he required surgery to restore his eyesight!

Track Star:

In May 2003, Albert Jackson Dowdy of Grants Pass, Oregon, was trying to break into a house. He found a first-floor window and used a can full of paint to break it. The window smashed and so did the can, spilling

paint all over the ground. The burglar got away with a can of tuna fish and a box of oatmeal. But on his way out, he stepped in the spilled paint. It didn't take long for the police to find him. All they had to do was follow the burglar's clearly defined footprints to the hotel where he was staying.

How Weird!

A panicked mother in Berlin, Germany, called on police to find her missing daughter. Police found the girl asleep, curled up . . .

a. in a haystack.
b. in the clothes dryer.
c. in a box that had been picked up that morning by a garbage truck.
d. under a pile of stuffed animals in her own bedroom.

Calling All Thieves:

Police investigating a burglary decided to try the number of a pager that had been stolen. It went off in the pocket of a man standing nearby—who was being questioned about a completely different crime.

43

Elvis Sighting: The year cabdriver Dave Groh of Seattle, Washington, dressed up as Elvis on Halloween, he enjoyed himself so much that he didn't feel like waiting another year to wear his costume. So he started dressing like Elvis every day. Groh says that not only did he enjoy his shtick but so did his passengers. In fact, he made a lot more in tips than he ever had before. Unfortunately, the costume didn't fit in with the city's cabdriver dress code, so he had to pay a $60 fine and stop wearing the Elvis outfit—at least, all but the cape!

How Weird!

At the University of Tennessee, the Body Farm consists of three acres of . . .

a. dormitories equipped with exercise machines to help people lose weight.
b. dead bodies in various stages of decomposition.
c. buildings with biofeedback machines to teach relaxation techniques.
d. corrals of cloned animals.

Freaky Forensics: The first thing you see when you enter the Forensic Museum in Bangkok, Thailand, is the museum's founder Songkran Nyomsane. Well, not him, exactly—just his skeleton. Continue on and you will see an assortment of body parts: bleeding brains, skulls with bullet holes, severed arms with tattoos, and a set of lungs with stab wounds. By far the main attraction is the mummy of a serial killer whose shriveled body slumps against a glass enclosure similar to a phone booth. You may want to time your visit so it's not too close to mealtime!

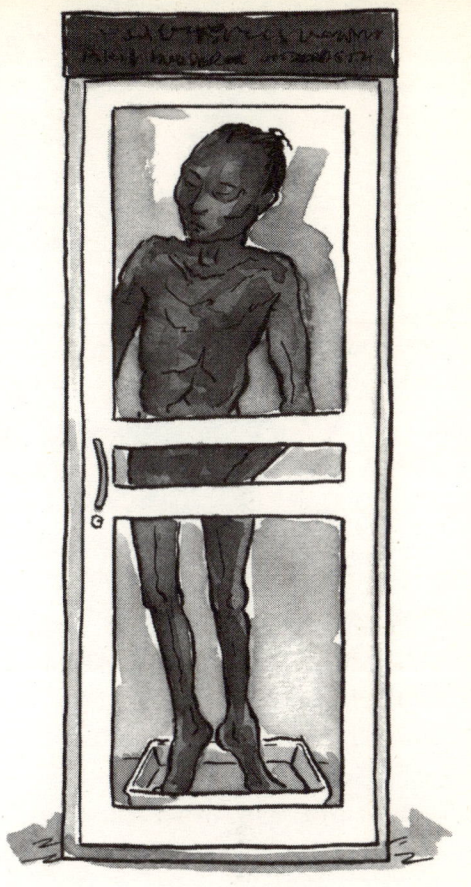

Museum of Madness: At Minnesota's Glore Psychiatric Museum, visitors can view such memorable exhibits as the contents found in a deceased patient's stomach—1,446 pieces of metal, including nails, hairpins, buttons, safety pins, screws, and bolts!

What a Croc! Soccer is not a particularly dangerous sport except when it's played by Erroberto Piza Rios. That's because Rios's teammates have huge jaws and sharp teeth. Rios entertains tourists at Playa Linda, a beach in the Ixtapa resort area in Mexico by kicking the ball around with crocodiles. For the price of a fish, the crocs let Rios balance the balls on their heads. One swift kick and Rios sends the ball from one croc's head to the neck of another, who casually lets the ball roll down its back. When the game is over, Rios stretches out on the back of a croc, scratches its belly, and gives it a kiss.

How Weird!

Authorities in Sweden denied a request by new parents to name their baby . . .

a. Valiant Viking.
b. The Hulk.
c. Superman.
d. The Terminator.

Web Site: New homeowners Susan and Andrew Parker had no idea they'd bought a comic book landmark—until they started getting mail that was addressed to Spider-Man! It seems their address in Forest Hills, New York, is the same as the comic book hero's. Not only that—the surname of Spider-Man's alter ego is Parker! Go figure!

No Baby on Board: Instead of landing instructions, pilots approaching England's Luton Airport heard the cries of a tiny baby coming loud and clear over their radios. After 12 hours of detective work, airline officials discovered that a baby monitor in a home near the airport was broadcasting the cries of little Freya Spratley to the cockpits of all approaching aircraft.

The Pits: When people living in Battle Mountain, Nevada, learned that their town was voted the "Armpit of the Nation" by the *Washington Post* newspaper, they decided not to make a big stink about it. Instead, with the sponsorship of Proctor & Gamble, the company that makes Old Spice products, they hosted the Old Spice Festival of the Pit, a big celebration featuring such attractions as the deodorant toss, the sweaty T-shirt contest, and the armpit beauty pageant. A stinky time was had by all.

How Weird!

For good luck, every night before a game, Mark Van Eeghen, a running back for the Oakland Raiders football team, . . .

a. wore 16 pairs of socks to bed.
b. balanced crackers on his nose.
c. dived from his television set to his bed.
d. wore his helmet to bed.

Bat-ty Behavior: Most athletes are a superstitious bunch, but baseball players are the most superstitious of all. To ward off bad luck, pitcher Turk Wendell brushes his teeth and chews licorice between every inning. Red Sox shortstop Nomar Garciaparra makes sure he touches every step with both feet when leaving the dugout and taps his toes during each time at bat. For good luck, many baseball players stick wads of gum on their bats or spit into their hands before picking them up. Hey, whatever works!

Curse of the Quarter: Shortly after their commemorative quarters were issued, several states had a run of bad luck. Right after New Hampshire's distinctive rock formation, known as the Old Man of the Mountain, was featured on the quarter, it crumbled to dust. Soon after Maryland's statehouse appeared on that state's quarter, it was struck by lightning. In Georgia, peach production suffered after a peach was featured on the state quarter, and the Vermont maple syrup industry suffered losses after being celebrated on the Vermont quarter. In fact, bad luck related to the images on their quarters has afflicted three out of every four states!

49

Fowl Festivities: At the annual Wayne Chicken Show held in July, residents of Wayne, Nebraska, can choose from a variety of events. For winged contestants, there is a best Chicken Song contest and a Most Beautiful Beak contest. Humans can compete in the Rubber Chicken Olympics or the National Cluck-Off contest—the person who sounds and acts the most like a chicken wins!

Half and Half: In the 1940s, John Pecinovsky of Iowa (*see cover*) liked to do things by halves. He wore clothes of different colors on each side of his body—and a different haircut and shave on each side of his head.

How Weird!

Jean Rath of Orcutt, California, lives in a purple house with purple appliances, wears only purple clothes, and owns a lilac . . .

a. bush.
b. car.
c. Siamese cat.
d. fake fur coat.

Some things that happen in real life are so weird that it would be hard to make them up. Can you tell the weird things that really happened from the one that's totally make-believe?

a. Inspired by the movie *Lord of the Rings*, Canadian Green Peace protesters wore stilts as they marched toward the British Columbia legislature building while chanting, "Save the trees."
Believe It!   Not!

b. The mental health department in Portland, Oregon, is looking for people fluent in Klingon, the language created for the *Star Trek* TV series. It seems that Klingon is the only language spoken by several mental patients in the county facility.
Believe It!   Not!

c. Queen Isabella of Spain used her pet parrot to judge the trustworthiness of visitors to the court. If the parrot squawked, the visitor was immediately banished to the New World.
Believe It!   Not!

d. In 1953, Frank Dyslin, Jr., and Betty Joy Anderson were married in Miami, Florida, while waterskiing.
Believe It!   Not!

BONUS QUESTION

Professor Bill Steed of Croaker College is . . .

a. an expert in frog psychology who uses hypnosis to train frogs to perform amazing feats like lifting barbells.

b. a doctor hired by rock stars because of his excellent record in curing laryngitis in just minutes.

c. an animal trainer whose 100-frog chorus performs all over the world.

d. a herpetologist who discovered that a substance secreted by a poison-dart frog kills pain 200 times faster than morphine.

When it comes to strange creations—from rock formations to weather phenomena—nothing is quite as unbelievable as nature's own works.

Soft Rock:

About 2,000 homes in Guadix, Spain, are caves carved into rock that is so soft it can be cut like cheese. Each home is equipped with electric lights and tiled floors. Their main advantage is that they seem to have a natural climate control that keeps residents warm in winter and cool in summer.

How Weird!

The amount of underground water in the United States is 50 times greater than all the water in . . .

a. the Atlantic Ocean.
b. the Mississippi River.
c. its rivers and streams combined.
d. Niagara Falls.

Fireworks: Trees and fields in Delburne, Alberta, Canada, began to spontaneously burst into flames in 1998 because of an underground fire in a coal bed that has been burning steadily for 140 years.

Totally Organic: The Great Stalacpipe Organ in the Luray Caverns of Virginia is the largest musical instrument in the world, covering 3.5 acres. Invented in 1954, the organ uses natural stalactites instead of metal pipes to make music. Its inventor, Leland Sprinkle, a mathematician and scientist, walked the caverns, deliberately choosing stalactites that would perfectly match the musical scale.

Nature's Xylophone: At Ringing Rocks State Park in Pennsylvania there is a 7-acre, 10-foot-deep pile of boulders. But these are not ordinary boulders. Tunes can be played on them by hitting stones of different pitch with a hammer.

Coal Coast: One of the most beautiful beaches in the world can be found in Hawaii, where turquoise waves crash over glistening jet-black sand made of disintegrated volcanic lava.

How Weird!

In 1943, Dionisio Pulido of Mexico lost his cornfield to . . .

a. a volcano that rose 160 feet in just 24 hours.
b. millions of locusts.
c. a cave-in caused by an earthquake.
d. thousands of crows.

Sand Show: In Mexico, there are mysterious columns of sand that appear suddenly and whirl violently—without the slightest breeze.

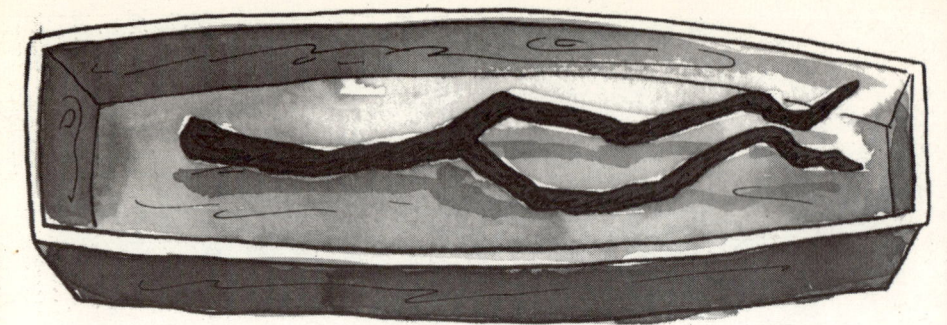

Rooting Around: When religious leader Roger Williams died in 1683, he was buried beside an apple tree in Providence, Rhode Island. The roots of the tree slowly absorbed his body and assumed a human shape!

Rock-etry: In 1916, ranchers drilling a well in Nevada accidentally pierced a vein of boiling hot water, and Fly Geyser has been gushing ever since. Over the years, minerals from the spouting water have built up, forming

three hills that look like 15-foot-high termite mounds. Their bright colors are produced by a combination of minerals, algae, and bacteria.

Animal Mania

Oh, Rats! Bowls of milk and food are scattered throughout the Karni Mata Temple in India for the rats that live there. Many people believe the rats carry the souls of storytellers and, when they die, will come back as people.

Polar Opposite: When Pelusa, a polar bear at a zoo in Argentina, developed a skin condition, veterinarians sprayed her with antiseptic that turned her white fur purple. Zoo-goers don't mind, but her male companion was so grumpy about it, he had to be moved.

Roach Infestation: Wingless Australian burrowing cockroaches are the biggest roaches in the world—and now they're being kept as pets in Australia.

Very Fishy: No, it's not a leaping fish. It's part of the National Fresh Water Fishing Hall of Fame in Wisconsin.

Have a Seat: An unwary guest would be quite surprised when he or she sat on a stool in the palace courtyard of Marcus Sitticus, a prince-archbishop in 17th-century Austria, and were blasted by a jet of water coming from underneath!

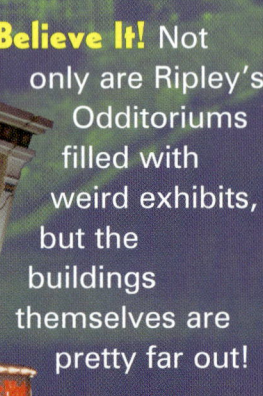

Believe It! Not only are Ripley's Odditoriums filled with weird exhibits, but the buildings themselves are pretty far out!

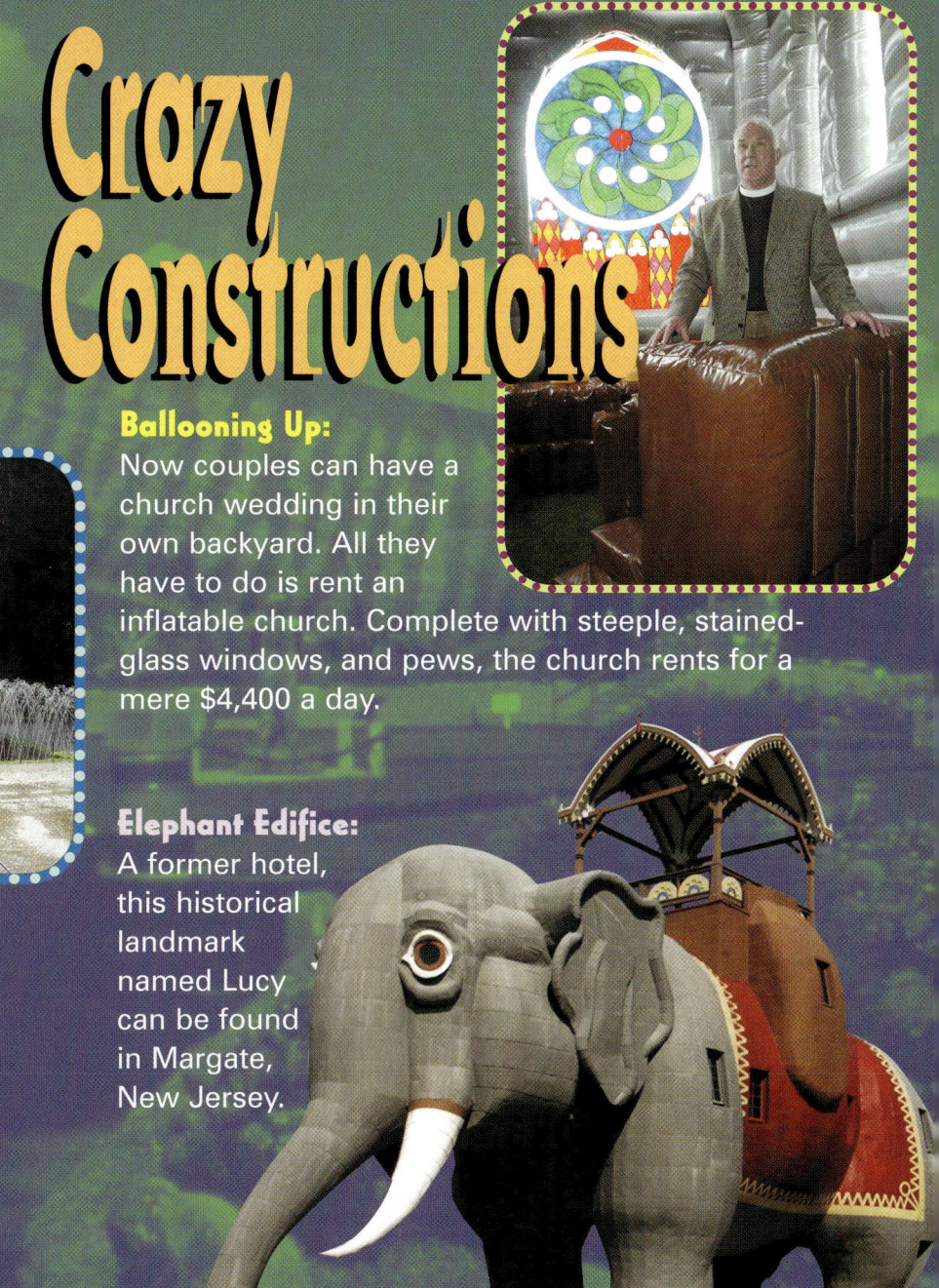

Crazy Constructions

Ballooning Up:
Now couples can have a church wedding in their own backyard. All they have to do is rent an inflatable church. Complete with steeple, stained-glass windows, and pews, the church rents for a mere $4,400 a day.

Elephant Edifice:
A former hotel, this historical landmark named Lucy can be found in Margate, New Jersey.

Going Wild

King of the Road:
After dressing up as Elvis one Halloween, cabdriver Dave Groh of Seattle, Washington, decided to wear his Elvis clothes every day. His tips improved, but he had to pay a fine for driving out of uniform.

Croc Stars: Erroberto Piza Rios entertains tourists at a beach in Mexico by playing soccer with crocodiles. He also holds some of the little fellows and lets them nibble on his face and arm.

A Little Behind in His Work:
Wearing only a cowboy hat, boots, and a pair of underpants, Robert John Burck is one street performer who gets a lot of attention.

All Shelled Out:
Camillo Russo of Australia loves seashells so much that he uses them to decorate his clothing and his home, which is covered with more than a million seashells!

Taking the Plunge: Everything about Chandan Thakoor and Dipti Pradhan's wedding was traditional—except the scuba gear they wore over their clothes so they could be married underwater.

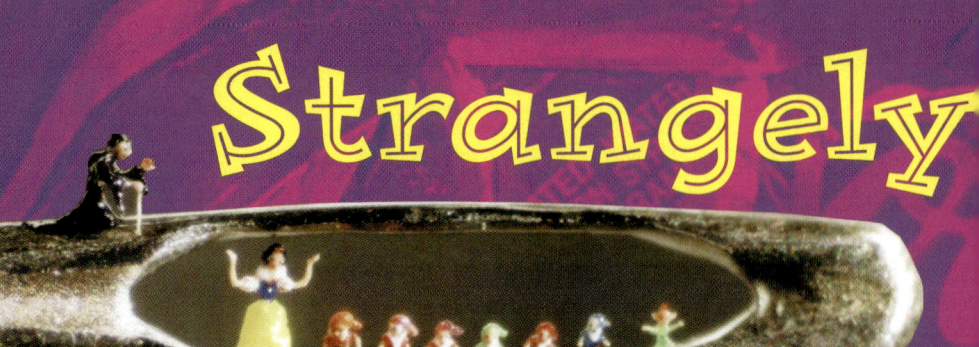

Strangely

Miniature Marvels: You would need a very good microscope to see the detail in Willard Wigan's sculpture of Snow White and the Seven Dwarfs perched in the eye of a sewing needle.

Skeleton in a Bottle: This miniature replica of the human skeleton was whittled out of wood by Clarence Pearson.

Match Shtick: Reg Pollard used more than a million matchsticks to build this replica of a 1907 Rolls Royce Silver Ghost.

Creative

Strung Out: Ken Butler
of New York creates such
unusual instruments as a
hubcap guitar and crutch bass.

Can You Believe?
Theresa Tozer
created this
life-sized metal
sculpture out
of flattened
soda cans.

Natural Wonders

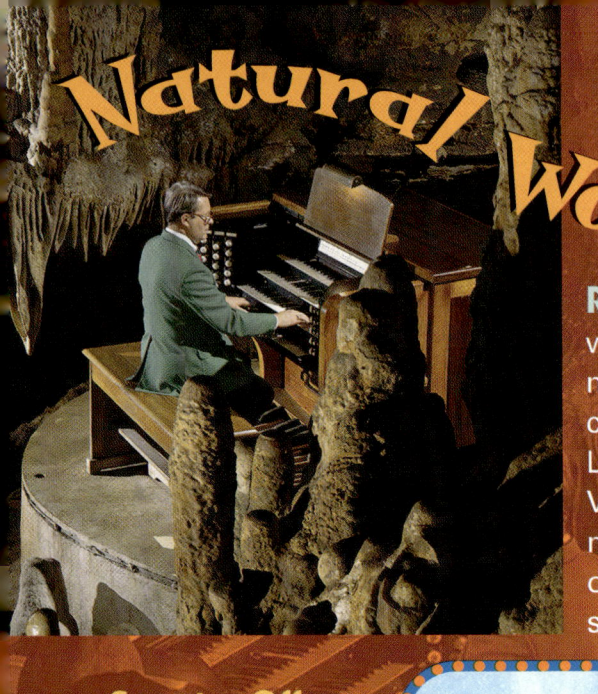

Rock Music: The world's largest musical instrument can be found in the Luray Caverns of Virginia. Instead of metal pipes, the organ uses natural stalactites.

Spouting Off: The bright colors of the Fly Geyser hills in Nevada are produced by a combination of minerals, algae, and bacteria.

Worth Its Salt: Lake Uyuni in Bolivia is the world's largest salt lake, but it's no more than 20 inches deep. Cloudlike salt formations jutting out of the azure water make it hard to tell the difference between lake and sky.

Gold Gush: In Antarctica, an active volcano spews pieces of pure gold when it erupts!

Hold the Onions: A hamburger-shaped rock formation in Cathedral Lakes Provincial Park, British Columbia, Canada, is for climbing, not eating.

How Weird!

Because Red Spring in Saint-Nectaire, France, has such a high sulfur content, anything thrown into its waters turns into . . .

a. red metal.
b. pink stone.
c. pink jelly.
d. red ashes.

Bedazzled: The snow funnels of the Himalayas are actually huge craters lined with iridescent green ice. The funnels have such a hypnotic effect that travelers feel an urge to leap into the dazzling pits.

Early Warning System: Seldom seen alive, the rare deep-sea oarfish helps scientists in Japan predict earthquakes. It seems that just prior to an earthquake, dead oarfish float to the surface from depths of more than 650 feet.

Light Show: A meteor shower on November 13, 1833, lit up the North American sky with 200,000 shooting stars.

Brown Out Down Under: A weird snowfall hit Australia in July 1935. A dust storm in the Mallee district and a snowstorm over the Victorian Alps caused chocolate-colored snow to fall at Mount Hotham.

How Weird!

The King Island, Alaska, New Year's Day Ice Bowl football game is always played on an ice floe but had to be canceled one year because . . .

a. the field melted.
b. a heavy snowfall caused the bleachers to collapse.
c. the field was blown away in a storm.
d. a herd of seals took over the ice floe.

Look Out Below!

During a severe hailstorm in Bovina, Mississippi, in 1876, one large hailstone was found to contain a 6-inch-long turtle.

Home Wrecker: A tornado carried away one end of a house without disturbing the dishes in the pantry.

Flaky! In 1887, huge snowflakes measuring 15 inches across and 8 inches thick fell over Fort Keogh, Montana.

Cliffhanger: A 267-foot-high cliff in the Tyrrhenian Sea is located 40 miles from the island of Sicily in Italy. To find out the weather forecast, Sicilians don't have to listen to the radio or television. All they have to do is look in the direction of the cliff. If they can see it, the weather is sure to remain fair.

How Weird!

All raindrops contain . . .

a. folic acid.
b. vitamin D.
c. algae.
d. vitamin B^{12}.

Many things that happen in nature are truly astonishing. Can you tell which of the following natural events are actually true and which one is astonishingly false?

a. Rainbows viewed from airplanes appear as complete circles.

Believe It!   **Not!**

b. After a flood in Hunter Valley, New South Wales, Australia, a small pig was found in half a pumpkin floating down the river. It had been eating the pumpkin as it sailed.

Believe It!   **Not!**

c. Wind blowing over the sand dunes in the Gobi Desert in Asia creates constant musical sounds that vary from a drumroll to a deep chant.

Believe It!   **Not!**

d. Tourists who drink from the Great Lake of Soda in East Africa say the water tastes exactly like hot chocolate.

Believe It!   **Not!**

BONUS QUESTION

In 1975, just before an earthquake struck in China, . . .

a. 50 pandas fled the forest and invaded Beijing.

b. hundreds of hibernating snakes mysteriously emerged from the ground.

c. the entire cat population began meowing at the same time.

d. thousands of birds began to fall out of the sky.

Whether for profit or just for fun, some people never run out of new ways to be creative.

How Weird!

A company in New York City makes a plastic and steel wallet that can only be opened with a four-digit code. If it's forced open, it . . .

a. spews paint.
b. emits a loud sirenlike noise.
c. self-destructs.
d. alerts the police via cell phone.

Cat Calls: Ever wonder what your cat's meows are telling you? The Meowlingual, a palm-sized electronic device, will provide you with a cat-a-log of the meaning of her every meow and purr.

Brown Bagging It: Anton Schiavone of Bangor, Pennsylvania, used paper grocery bags to build a life-sized replica of Leonardo Da Vinci's *Last Supper*.

Scent-sational: Kanebo, a cosmetic company in Japan, has developed a line of pantyhose that are embedded with vitamins and special scents that are released when worn.

Sun Dial: A wristwatch on sale in the United States warns wearers when they are in danger of getting a sunburn.

Junkyard Band: A hubcap guitar and crutch bass are just two of the unusual instruments created by Ken Butler of upstate New York. All are playable.

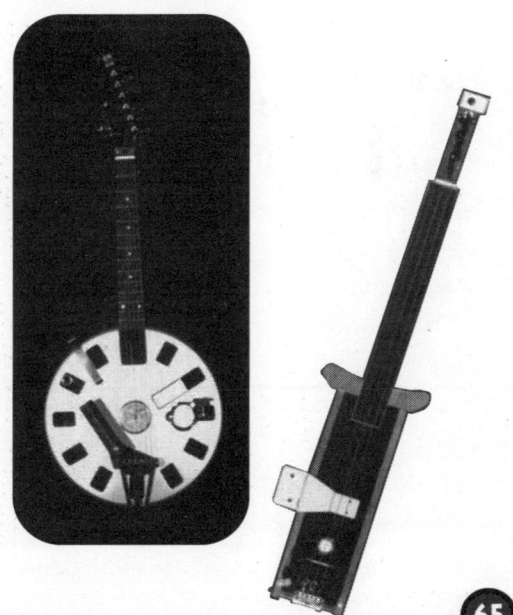

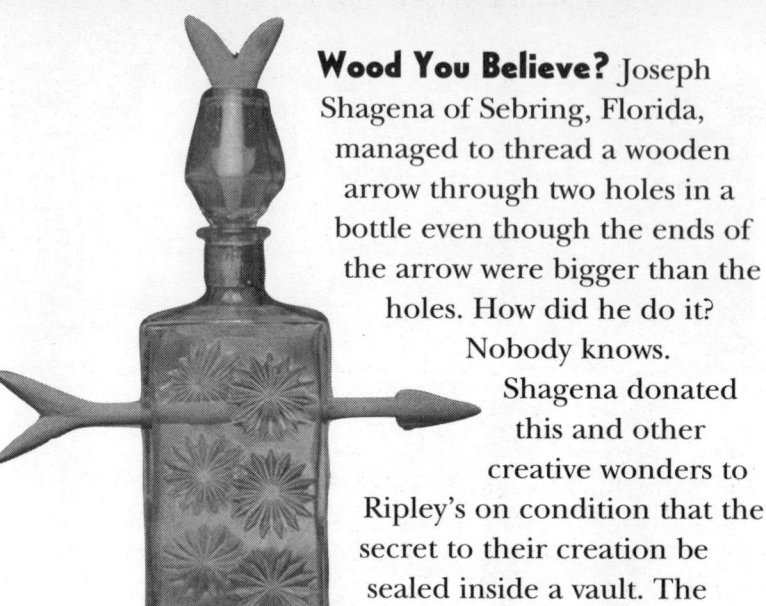

Wood You Believe? Joseph Shagena of Sebring, Florida, managed to thread a wooden arrow through two holes in a bottle even though the ends of the arrow were bigger than the holes. How did he do it? Nobody knows.

Shagena donated this and other creative wonders to Ripley's on condition that the secret to their creation be sealed inside a vault. The secret remains locked away to this day.

Eye Strain: That's what Harold Blahnik of Kewanee, Wisconsin, must have had after threading an ordinary sewing needle with 93 strands of thread.

Chain Reaction: Robert Ripley was so impressed with the continuous chain whittled by H. T. Stewart from a single 20-foot by 1-foot plank that he used himself to display it.

How Weird!

In 1940, Wilma Beth Shulke of Mission, Texas, put together an outfit made from the cross sections of . . .

a. corncobs and orange peels.
b. acorns and squash gourds.
c. peach pits and bamboo shoots.
d. apple cores and corn kernels.

A Real Brick:

Albert Whitworth sketched every single one of the 800,000 bricks in the 13-mile-long, 1,600-year-old Hadrian's Wall in northern England. Sketching at a rate of $5/8$ of a mile every 16 months, he took 13 years to complete his project.

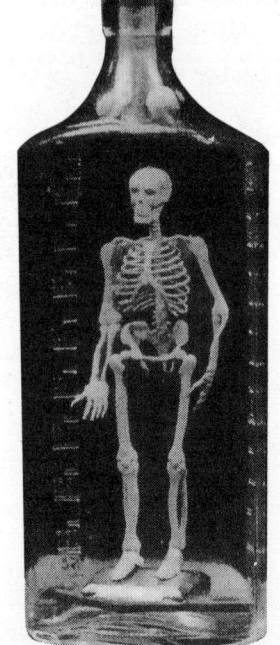

Match Shtick: In 1983, Reg Pollard built a replica of a 1907 Rolls Royce Silver Ghost out of more than one million matchsticks.

Wooden Expression: Clarence Pearson of Mount Vernon, Illinois, whittled a miniature replica of every bone in the human skeleton out of wood, then painstakingly assembled them inside a bottle.

Saving Soles: French artist Dominique Bordenave creates sculptures out of old shoes.

Shedding Light:
In Quemado, New Mexico, there is a Christmas tree made out of approximately 700 elk antlers covered with pretty lights.

Portrait Puncher: Aric Obrosey of New York City uses a knife and a hole punch to create lacelike rubber portraits of famous people.

Square Deal: In 1955, the Quaker Oats Company of Canada placed legal deeds to one square inch of land in the Canadian Yukon inside their boxes of Puffed Rice and Puffed Wheat.

How Weird!

In Takasaki, Japan, there is a phone booth built in the shape of a huge . . .

a. sushi roll.
b. bass fiddle.
c. baseball bat.
d. shark.

Going Buggy: Based on the premise that there's no roach like a dead roach, the Cockroach Hall of Fame Museum exhibits the dead bugs dressed up in costumes and posed in mini dioramas. Liberoachi *(above)* and Marilyn Monroach are two museum-goer favorites.

Coin of a Kind: No one would ever guess that an ordinary-looking penny has a slide-out drawer with a photograph of the famous collector of miniatures, Jules Charbneau, inside.

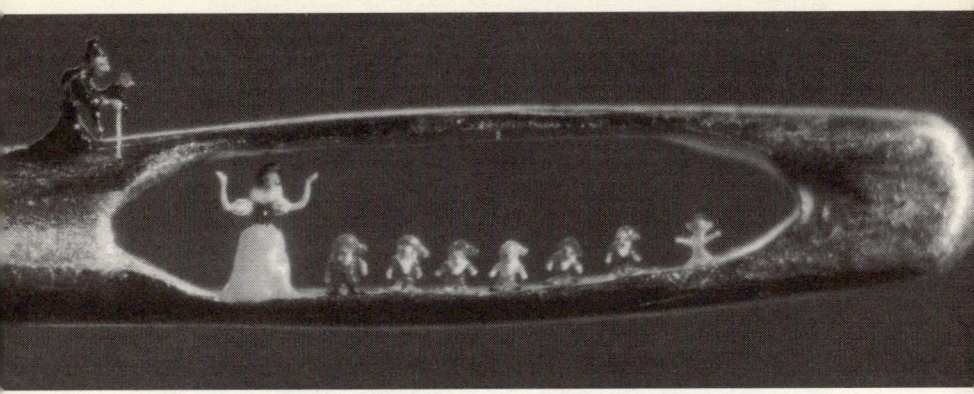

Miniature Marvels: Willard Wigan's sculptures are invisible to the naked eye. You need a very good microscope to see his Snow White and the Seven Dwarfs perched in the eye of a sewing needle, his copy of Mount Rushmore on the sharp tip of a pencil, or his polar bear sitting on a single granule of sugar. Microsurgeons come from far and wide to observe Willard in his studio, hoping to learn the secret of his supersteady hands. These microsculptures may be seen by visiting the Impossible MicroWorld Museum in Bath, England.

Throne Room: Jeweler Lam Sai-wing of Hong Kong created the Rolls-Royce of toilets. Made out of solid gold, it is the centerpiece of a lavish bathroom whose ceiling is encrusted with rubies, sapphires, and emeralds.

How Weird!

Norman Kautz, of Texas City, Texas, builds model ships inside . . .

a. bottles.
b. conch shells.
c. teacups.
d. light bulbs.

Colossal Collage: Standing 25 feet tall and 20 feet wide, this reproduction of Vincent van Gogh's famous self-portrait was created by Dutch artist Cornel Bierens from 3,000 postcards, each featuring a painting by van Gogh.

How Weird!

During the 19th century, popular toys for children included . . .

a. miniature trolley cars.
b. miniature guillotines.
c. dolls made out of bug casings.
d. pull toys made out of coconuts.

Here are some super amazing products that are downright weird. Can you tell which one is purely an invention of the imagination?

a. In 1992, Kenji Kawakami of Japan created padded booties for cats to dust the floor with.
Believe It!   Not!

b. An American kitchen design company builds fantasy kitchens complete with appliances that operate by the sound of human voices.
Believe It!   Not!

c. Miniature lamps filled with a superstrain of fireflies from the West Indies emit a glow that is bright enough to read by.
Believe It!   Not!

d. American jigsaw puzzle maker Steve Richardson often puts extra pieces in the boxes that don't fit anywhere in the puzzle.
Believe It!   Not!

BONUS QUESTION

A company in the United States has invented an inflatable sofa for outdoor use that . . .

a. buzzes when it's time to apply sunscreen.

b. squirts water to cool off its occupant.

c. releases mosquito repellent every 20 minutes.

d. changes color when it's about to rain.

POP QUIZ

Weird trivia test! Here's your chance to prove how well acquainted you've become with the weird side of life—everything you've just read in this book!

1. If parents in the Ozark Mountains wanted their child to be a good dancer, it was once the custom to . . .
a. play music for the baby while it was still in the womb.
b. dance around the baby's crib five times.
c. sprinkle sugar on the baby's feet.
d. squash the first louse they found on the baby's head.

2. Instead of throwing rice at weddings during the Middle Ages, people threw . . .
a. eggs.
b. old shoes.
c. tomatoes.
d. confetti.

3. In Southeast Asia, coconuts are often harvested by . . .
a. ferrets.
b. house cats.
c. monkeys.
d. rats.

4. In 1891, a British nobleman built a giant pigsty in the shape of a Greek temple.

Believe It!   **Not!**

5. During the 17th century, prince-archbishop Marcus Sitticus of Salzburg, Austria, had water jets installed on the stools around his palace courtyard to . . .

a. serve as birdbaths.

b. water the nearby flowers.

c. discourage stray cats from perching on them.

d. surprise his guests.

6. Within the dome of India's Gol-Gumbaz, there is a room called the Whispering Gallery where . . .

a. it is against the law to speak above a whisper.

b. the acoustics are so good that whispers are amplified to shouts.

c. whispered secrets remain in the walls, echoing long after the teller has left.

d. the sound of laughter produces more echoes than any other kind of sound.

7. To protest his arrest at Athens International Airport, Remi Tsolakis . . .

a. stood on his head.

b. chained himself to the ticket counter.

c. popped his eyeballs out of his head.

d. sang the Greek National Anthem.

8. One of the most popular attractions at Thailand's Forensic Museum is . . .

a. an Egyptian mummy.

b. a shrunken head.

c. a two-headed calf.

d. a mummified serial killer.

9. Homeowners Susan and Andrew Parker of Forest Hills, New York, started getting letters addressed to Superman.

Believe It!   **Not!**

10. In 1999, trees and fields in Alberta, Canada, began bursting into flames due to . . .

a. the activity of underground volcanoes.

b. sparks from a nearby incinerator.

c. a fire in an underground coal bed.

d. careless campers.

11. The hills built up by Fly Geyser in Nevada are brightly colored due to . . .

a. mineral, algae, and bacteria deposits.

b. graffiti artists.

c. reflected rainbows produced by the sun shining on the geyser.

d. windswept particles from a paint factory that exploded miles from the site.

12. Deep-sea oarfish in Japan help scientists predict earthquakes by . . .
a. floating to the surface.
b. turning colors.
c. giving off a radiant glow.
d. producing a buzzing noise.

13. Anton Schiavone built a life-sized replica of Leonardo Da Vinci's *Last Supper* using only plastic grocery bags.

Believe It!   **Not!**

14. French artist Dominique Bordenave creates sculptures out of . . .
a. laundry lint.
b. crushed seashells.
c. old shoes.
d. papier-mâché.

15. A cosmetic company in Japan makes pantyhose that . . .
a. are embedded with vitamins and special fragrances.
b. are made with spider webs for extra strength.
c. are embedded with tiny diamonds to make them sparkle.
d. turn light or dark depending on the time of day.

Answer Key

Chapter 1
Curious Customs
Page 5:   **c.** draw the most worms out of the ground.
Page 7:   **d.** plant their crops in boats set high above the ground.
Page 9:   **a.** cabbage.
Page 11: **a.** cows' horns.
Page 13: **a.** had to climb on a raised platform to get into them.
Page 14: **a.** squeezed into a jar and kept there for a year.
Page 16: **b.** wearing pants in public.
Page 19: **b.** shamans would not burn.
Page 20: **a.** it's illegal to own a dog in China.
Brain Buster: b. is false.
Bonus Question: c. pencils.

Chapter 2
Astonishing Structures
Page 23: **c.** bundles of rushes.
Page 25: **a.** old houses were burned down to recover them.
Page 27: **a.** stolen.
Page 29: **d.** one fingernail.
Page 30: **c.** mammoth bones.
Page 32: **a.** in the United States and the kitchen in Canada.
Page 34: **c.** block his next-door neighbor's view.
Brain Buster: b. is false.
Bonus Question: b. is entirely covered with 24-carat gold.

Chapter 3
Totally Out There

Page 37:   **b.** race in which competitors pull wooden outhouses through the snow.

Page 39:   **a.** carried bouquets of garlic, chives, and rosemary.

Page 41:   **a.** Dracula theme park.

Page 43:   **d.** under a pile of stuffed animals in her own bedroom.

Page 44:   **b.** dead bodies in various stages of decomposition.

Page 46:   **c.** Superman.

Page 48:   **c.** dived from his television set to his bed.

Page 50:   **c.** Siamese cat.

Brain Buster: c. is false.

Bonus Question: a. an expert in frog psychology who uses hypnosis to train frogs to perform amazing feats like lifting barbells.

Chapter 4
Naturally Peculiar

Page 53:   **c.** its rivers and streams combined.

Page 55:   **a.** a volcano that rose 160 feet in just 24 hours.

Page 57:   **b.** pink stone.

Page 58:   **c.** the field was blown away in a storm.

Page 60:   **d.** vitamin B^{12}.

Brain Buster: d. is false.

Bonus Question: b. hundreds of hibernating snakes mysteriously emerged from the ground.

Chapter 5
Outrageous Stuff

Page 63: **c.** self-destructs.

Page 64: **c.** coconut.

Page 67: **a.** corncobs and orange peels.

Page 69: **b.** bass fiddle.

Page 71: **d.** light bulbs.

Page 72: **b.** miniature guillotines.

Brain Buster: c. is false.

Bonus Question: b. squirts water to cool off its occupant.

Pop Quiz

1. **d.**
2. **a.**
3. **c.**
4. **Believe It!**
5. **d.**
6. **d.**
7. **c.**
8. **d.**
9. **Not!**
10. **c.**
11. **a.**
12. **a.**
13. **Not!**
14. **c.**
15. **a.**

What's Your Ripley's Rank?

Ripley's Scorecard

Way to go! You've made it to the end of the Ripley's weird world of fabulous facts and strange tales. Now it's time to rate yourself. Are you a **Wizard of Weird** or a plain, old **Normal Mortal**? Check out the answers in the answer key, and use this page to keep track of how many trivia questions you've answered correctly. Then all you have to do is add up your score to find out your rank.

Here's the scoring breakdown. Give yourself:
★ **10 points** for every **How Weird!** question you answered correctly;
★ **20 points** for every fiction you spotted in the **Ripley's Brain Busters**;
★ **10 points** every time you fielded a **Bonus Question**;
★ and **5 points** for every **Pop Quiz** question you got right.

Here's a tally sheet:
Number of **How Weird!**
questions answered correctly: _____ x 10 = _____
Number of **Ripley's Brain Buster**
fictions spotted: _____ x 20 = _____
Number of **Bonus Questions**
you fielded: _____ x 10 = _____
Number of **Pop Quiz** questions
answered correctly: _____ x 5 = _____

Total the right column for your final score: _____

0–100
Normal Mortal

Wild and weird is just not your thing. You take pride in appearing normal and have a deep appreciation for the average. But one day you might discover that there's another whole world out there—a world of extremes. Furthermore, you just may find out that wacky and weird can be downright entertaining!

101–250
Strangely Off

Your antennae for weird stuff needs some adjustment. Stories about people dancing with dead relatives may not be your cup of tea. The good news is you've shown just enough aptitude for distinguishing the made-up stories from the factual ones that you shouldn't give up. Just remember that some true stories are often stranger by far than fiction!

251–400
Wild and Freaky

You have a keen appreciation for the weird side of life. Once in a while, a phony fact will slip by you, but that's just because you have such a vivid imagination. Most of the time, though, you're right on the mark. If there's even a remote chance for you to attend a weird event such as a soccer game with crocodiles as players, you will make sure not to miss it.

401–575
Wizard of Weird

You must really get around! You've done an extra-
oddinary job of spotting the bogus facts among all the
incredibly weird but true ones. You did so well in the
How Weird! quizzes that you must have a built-in
lie detector!

Believe It!®

Photo Credits

Ripley Entertainment Inc. and the editors of this book wish to thank the following photographers, agents, and other individuals for permission to use and reprint the following photographs in this book. Any photographs included in this book that are not acknowledged below are property of the Ripley Archives. Great effort has been made to obtain permission from the owners of all materials included in this book. Any errors that may have been made are unintentional and will gladly be corrected in future printings if notice is sent to Ripley Entertainment Inc., 5728 Major Boulevard, Orlando, Florida 32819.

Black & White Photos

7 Helicopter Herding Cattle/© Yann Arthus-Bertrand/CORBIS

8 Fingernail Money Fashion/Atif Toor

10 Yellow Oleander/Anthony P. Knight, from "A Guide to Plant Poisoning of Animals in North America," copyright 2001 Teton New Media

12 Makeup/Laura Miller

14 Maori with Tattoos/Frans Lanting Photography/www.lanting.com

17 Aborigine/© Corbis Images/PictureQuest

18 Butterfly/© Corel Images

23 Great Wall of China/Ablestock

24 Leonardo Bridge/Terje Johannsen/See Also www.vebjorn-sand.com

26 Lucy/Courtesy of the Save Lucy Committee/www.lucytheelephant.org

27 Grand Mosque of Djenné/Andrew Gilham/www.andygilham.com

28 Koutoubia Tower/World Religions Photo Library/www.worldreligions.co.uk

31 National Fresh Water Fishing Hall of Fame/Courtesy National Fresh Water Fishing Hall of Fame

33 Building in Odeillo, France/Gerhard Weinrebe

38 Underwater Wedding Ceremony/Sherwin Crasto/Reuters Pictures Archive

41 Karni Mata Temple/Kamal Kishore/Reuters Pictures Archive

47 Spider-Man/Bender/Helper Impact

53 Guadix, Spain/Peter Hill and Linda Pan

54 Luray Caverns/Courtesy of Luray Caverns

56 Fly Geyser/Lee Baca

70 Cockroach Exhibit/Courtesy Cockroach Hall of Fame

71 Willard Wigan Sculpture/Art International Management

Color Insert

(1) Karni Mata Temple/Kamal Kishore/ Reuters Pictures Archive; Pelusa/Paula Paez/Reuters Pictures Archive; Cockroach Pet/David Gray/Reuters Pictures Archive

(2–3) National Fresh Water Fishing Hall of Fame/Courtesy National Fresh Water Fishing Hall of Fame; Trick Fountains/Foto Sulzer/ All Rights: Schloss Hellbrunn, A-5020 Salzburg; Inflatable Church/Toby Melville/Reuters Pictures Archive; Lucy/Courtesy of the Save Lucy Committee/www.lucytheelephant.org

(4–5) Dave Groh/Alan Berner/KRT; Erroberto Piza Rios/Daniel Aguilar/Reuters Pictures Archive; Robert John Burck/Naked Cowboy/© Jim Richards; Underwater Wedding/Sherwin Crasto/Reuters Pictures Archive

(6–7) Willard Wigan Sculpture/Art International Management

(8) Luray Caverns/Courtesy of Luray Caverns; Fly Geyser/Lee Baca; Lake Uyuni/PEPITA/ CORBIS SYGMA

Cover

Mud Men of Asaro/Miriam Nadel; Fly Geyser/Lee Baca

WE'D LOVE TO BELIEVE YOU!

Do you have a Believe It or Not!
story that has happened to you or to someone
you know? If it's weird enough and if you would
like to share it, the people at Ripley's would love
to hear about it. You can send your
Believe It or Not! entries to:

The Director of the Archives
Ripley Entertainment Inc.
5728 Major Boulevard
Orlando, Florida 32819

Believe It!®